To my daughter, Bria, my very own nose-biting monster.
- Jay

To my wife, Sandra, and my son, Luis, for being there for me and allowing me
to keep doing this stuff when I should be getting "a real job"
instead, like regular people seem to do...
- Luis

New Paige Press, LLC
NewPaigePress.com

New Paige Press and the distinctive ladybug icon are registered trademarks of New Paige Press, LLC

Copyedited by Amanda Brodkin

ISBN 978-0-692-09269-9

Printed and bound in China

New Paige Press provides special discounts when purchased in larger volumes for premiums
and promotional purposes, as well as for fundraising and educational use. Custom editions can
also be created for special purposes. In addition, suplemental teaching material can be provided
upon request. For more information, please contact sales@newpaigepress.com.

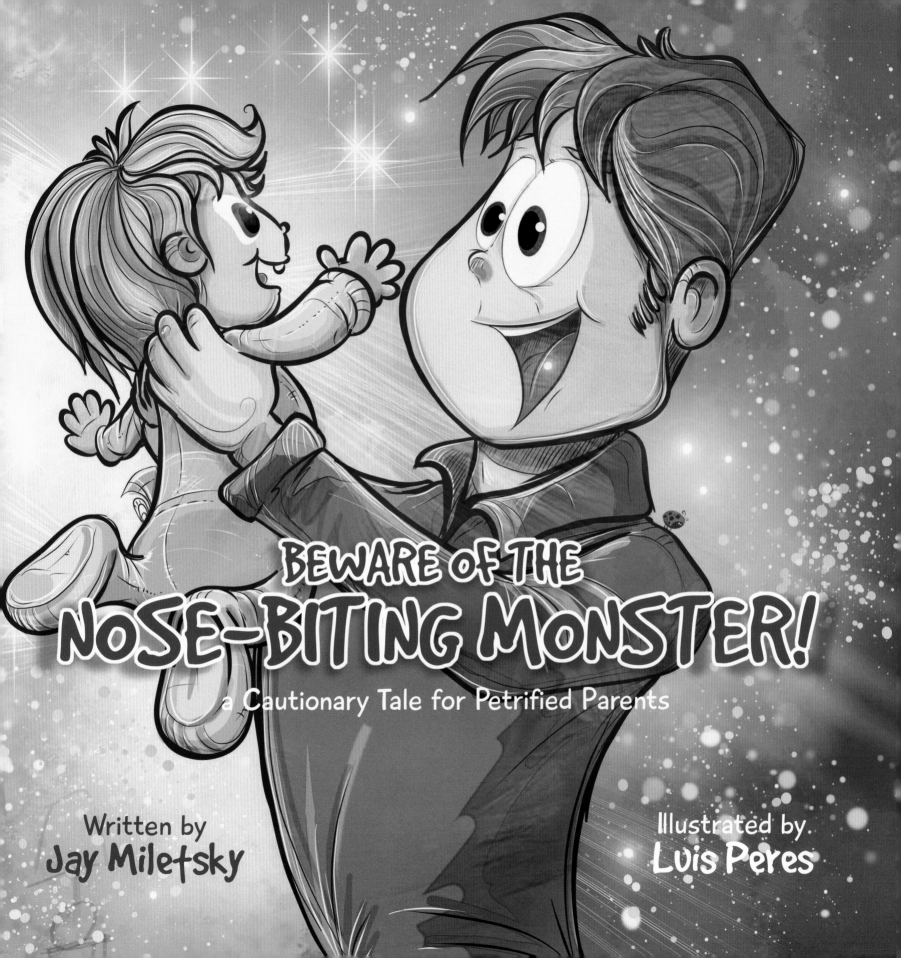

BEWARE OF THE NOSE-BITING MONSTER!

a Cautionary Tale for Petrified Parents

Written by
Jay Miletsky

Illustrated by
Luis Peres

It might sound made-up, or far-fetched at least,
but this is the story of a terrible beast,
who surprised me one day when, quite unannounced,
it gazed at my face and then suddenly pounced,
chomping down hard with a loud, high-pitched squeal,
and mistaking my nose for a fine, gourmet meal!

I had no idea, not even a clue,
when it suddenly bit me from out of the blue,
that my sweet little kid would turn suddenly wild
and grow into a dangerous, nose-biting child!

You see, when it was younger it was cute as a button,
but one day teeth appeared, and then all of a sudden,
its appetite grew for one thing, I suppose:
it wanted to feast on the flesh of my nose!

At first it would nibble — it was really quite cute —
gnawing my nose like a booger-filled fruit.

But one day that all changed, when I couldn't entice
it to loosen a bite that clamped down like a vice,
and left my poor nose chewed, gnarled, and raw.
So from that day on I quite clearly saw,
that I'd have to protect the end of my snout,
whenever my nose-biting monster's about.

It hides in the corners, and prepares with a smirk,
to bite me the moment I come home from work.
Or it creeps 'round behind in a stealth sneak attack,
licking its lips 'fore its next late night snack.

Sometimes it can trick me (and this works every time)
by looking real sweet and then trying to climb
up into my arms to give me a hug
and curl into my chest, all cuddled and snug…

But the truth is it has a devious plot,
to chew where I keep my treasure of snot.
It pretends that it wants my cheek for a kiss,
but I suddenly realize that something's amiss!

Too late! It gets me, and chomps hard on my beak,
leaving me howling in pain for a week!
It jumps up and down, ignoring my cries,
but does not realize that I've got a surprise...

I've figured out how I could end this for good,
so my monster will act the way all monsters should...

The one, surefire way to get out of this pickle
is to give my fierce nose-biter

A BIG MONSTER TICKLE!

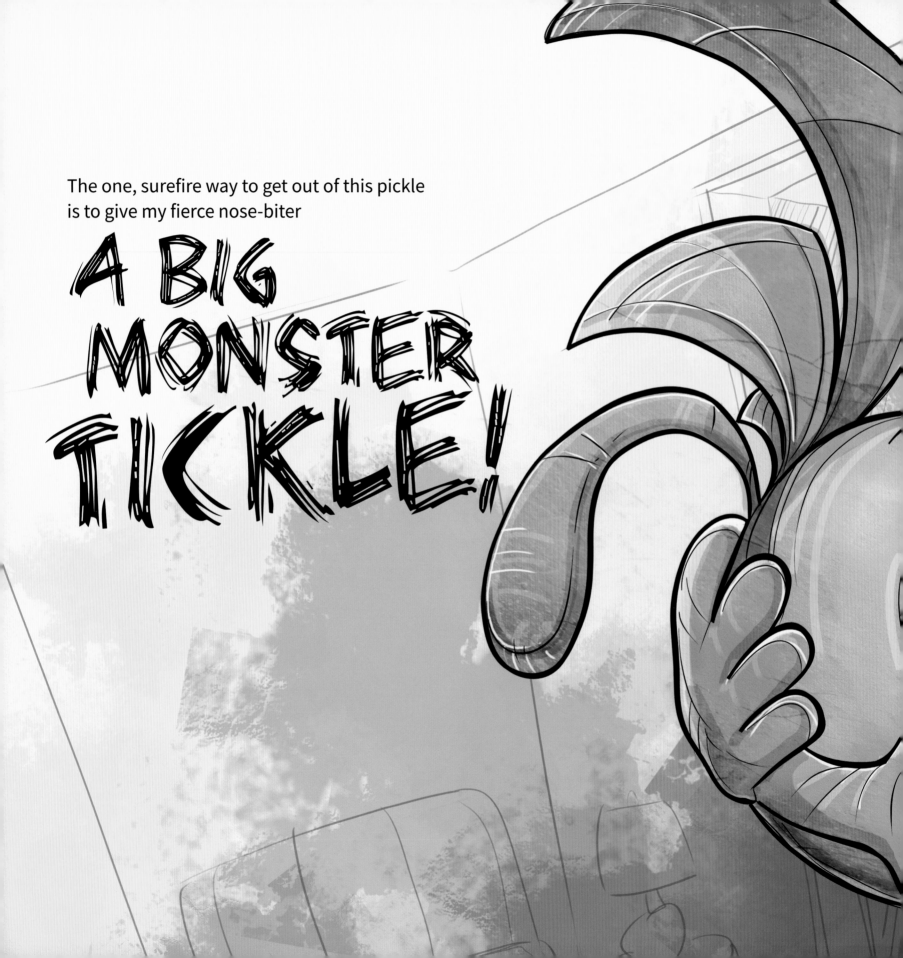

So parents please hear me — take my warning to heart,
you need to beware and prepared from the start.
There are all sorts of ways kids express how they feel,
some give you a hug...others make you a meal.
Not everyone uses their voice as a clue...
Some monsters bite — to say,

"I LOVE YOU!"